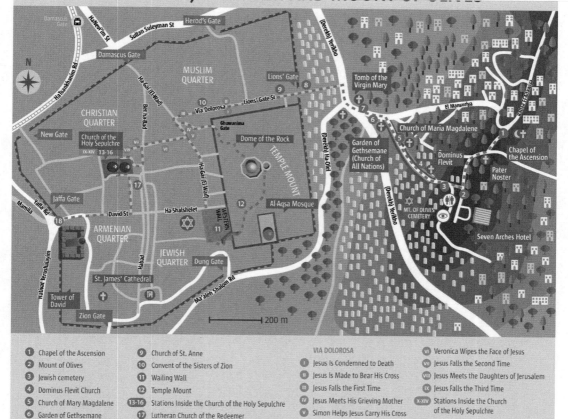

OLD CITY OF JERUSALEM AND MOUNT OF OLIVES

- ❶ Chapel of the Ascension
- ❷ Mount of Olives
- ❸ Jewish cemetery
- ❹ Dominus Flevit Church
- ❺ Church of Mary Magdalene
- ❻ Garden of Gethsemane
- ❼ Tomb of the Virgin Mary
- ❽ Lions' Gate – Old City
- ❾ Church of St. Anne
- ❿ Convent of the Sisters of Zion
- ⓫ Wailing Wall
- ⓬ Temple Mount
- 13-16 Stations Inside the Church of the Holy Sepulchre
- ⓱ Lutheran Church of the Redeemer
- ⓲ Jaffa Gate

VIA DOLOROSA
- Ⅰ Jesus Is Condemned to Death
- Ⅱ Jesus Is Made to Bear His Cross
- Ⅲ Jesus Falls the First Time
- Ⅳ Jesus Meets His Grieving Mother
- Ⅴ Simon Helps Jesus Carry His Cross
- Ⅵ Veronica Wipes the Face of Jesus
- Ⅶ Jesus Falls the Second Time
- Ⅷ Jesus Meets the Daughters of Jerusalem
- Ⅸ Jesus Falls the Third Time
- Ⅹ-ⅩⅣ Stations Inside the Church of the Holy Sepulchre

▬▬▬▬ Old City wall ▪ ▪ ▪ ▪ ▪ Tour route 👁 Lookout 🚻 Toilets

Introduction

Jerusalem is Israel's poorest city. It is suffused with religion and often choked with dust, and it can be harsh and unpleasant. But there is no equal to Jerusalem in terms of historical, cultural, and religious treasures. This booklet focuses on the main religious sites on the Mount of Olives and in the Old City. If you visit them all in one day (don't worry, there's no need to rush), you'll be tired but rewarded with the experience of touring nothing less than the historical and religious foundations of Western civilization.

My name is Oren Cahanovitc and, as a traveler and a tour guide who has introduced hundreds of travelers to the magic of Jerusalem, I will sum up its long and tumultuous history without burdening you with too many details, while still taking you through the highlights of this unique and fascinating city.

Please note:

Modest clothing – We will visit holy sites on the tour, so please make sure that your elbows, cleavage, and knees are covered. A head covering is not necessary.

Visiting the Temple Mount – It is prohibited to visit the Temple Mount while carrying large religious symbols, Bibles, or prayer books. It is also forbidden to bring alcohol or any sharp or dangerous objects, such as knives and firearms.

Bible – Unless you wish to visit the Temple Mount (where it is prohibited), it is recommended to bring a Bible along. When you read from the Bible while visiting holy sites, many things become clearer and sometimes interesting questions arise.

Opening hours – Some of the sites are closed during the afternoon, and visiting the Temple Mount is only allowed during certain hours.

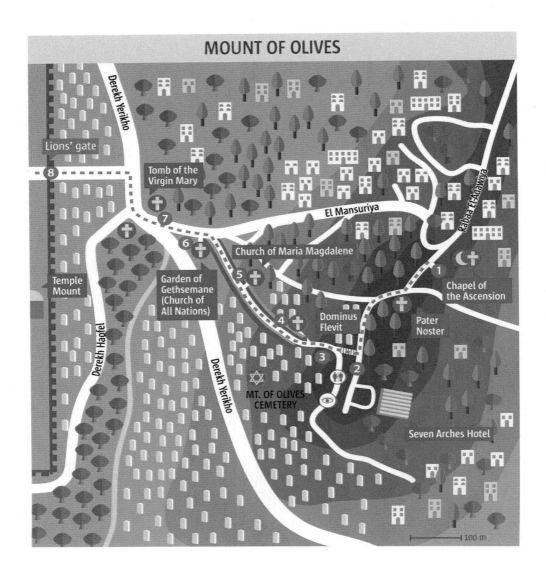

Holy Geography

Many churches that you will visit today are not beautiful in the classical sense. The churches in Europe are much more impressive than the ones you will see in Jerusalem, but those in the holy city were built on sites that are related to the story of Jesus. Only here can you read from the New Testament, point to a rock, and say, "This is the place!"

On this tour, you will see Christ's footprint in the place from which he ascended to heaven, and you will visit the exact place where he is believed to have been crucified. If you have the patience to wait in a long line, you'll be able to see where he was buried and where he rose back to life. You will visit the stone upon which Christ prayed the night before his crucifixion and the three places where he fell under the weight of the cross on his way to Golgotha.

How do we know that these are really the exact places? (This is often asked by people who are skeptical by nature.) No one can know for sure, because Jerusalem has been destroyed and rebuilt many times since Christ walked here, and the specific sites where events took place were not mentioned in the New Testament.

Mark Twain, who visited the Land of Israel in 1867, wrote, "Wherever they [Catholics] ferret out a lost locality made holy by some Scriptural event, they straightway build a massive - almost imperishable - church there, and preserve the memory of that locality for the gratification of future generations. If it had been left to Protestants to do this most worthy work, we would not even know where Jerusalem is today."

Of course, Mark Twain was being cynical, but he was referring to a phenomenon more common in Christian practice than in Judaism or in Islam - Holy Geography. Almost every church, monastery, and chapel in Jerusalem is somehow connected to the life of Christ. Are the rocks you can see in the churches really the places where Christ worked his wonders? The answer is: It doesn't matter. It's a question of faith. The close connection between the life of Christ and the geography of Jerusalem is one of the ways Christian believers relate to Christ's story and life.

1. The Chapel (Mosque) of the Ascension

Opening hours: It's open most of the day. If it's closed when you visit, you can knock on the door of the adjacent mosque and ask to be let in.
Entrance fee: NIS 5-10.
Directions: There is no public transportation to the site. The best way to get there is by foot or taxi, which costs around NIS 50-70 from the city center.

The tour begins in a place that seems unremarkable, but is actually one of the holiest places to Christians on the Mount of Olives. This is where Jesus ascended to heaven.
Christ lived on the Mount of Olives during the last week of his life. He was crucified and buried on a Friday (in the place where the Church of the Holy Sepulchre stands today). On Sunday, his coffin was found empty. Jesus walked on Earth for another forty days and rose to heaven from this spot.

On top of the site where a church dating back from the 4th century stood, the Crusaders built an octagonal, fortified church. Today, only the outer walls and the aedicule, a small octagon-shaped building in the center of the site, remain. On the floor of the building, you can

The Chapel of the Ascension

see a stone with Christ's footprint. After the Muslims conquered the place in 1187, they converted the church into a mosque, which is why the place has two names - the Mosque of the Ascension or the Church (or Chapel) of the Ascension. The Muslims do not believe that Christ is the son of God but do recognize him as an important prophet, which is why they turned the church into a mosque. In the Crusaders' church, the stone containing the footprint of Christ was in the center of the room, but after it became a mosque, the Muslims moved the stone a couple of centimeters southward toward the direction of Mecca - the direction to which they pray.

Today, the place enjoys a special status - it is usually used as a mosque except on the day that Christians mark Jesus' ascension to heaven; for that one day, it becomes a church. This is the only place in the world that serves as both a church and a mosque.

Close to the Chapel of the Ascension, there is a mosque that is built upon a cemetery plot (entrance to non-Muslims is forbidden). You will receive a multitude of answers to the question, "Who is buried there?" Jews will tell you that it is Huldah, a prophetess. Muslims will say that it is the grave of Raba el-Adiwa, a Muslim mystic. Christians will tell you that it is the grave of Saint Pelagia, a harlot-turned-nun. She was a beautiful girl who lived a life of sin until she repented of her ways, disguised herself as a man, and lived as a monk. Only after her death was her identity discovered (the story of repentant promiscuous women is common among Christians). So who is really buried here? A Jewish prophetess, a Muslim mystic, or a Christian nun? This is a question of faith. The interesting fact is that followers of the three religions believe that this place is the burial site of an important woman. One of the more admirable and

persistent motifs in Jerusalem is that no matter who the ruler is – and the city has chang
hands quite a few times – the same sites are considered holy and many of their attributes do
not change.

2. Mount of Olives Observation Point
Always open; free entrance; public restroom on site

In the morning hours, with the sun at your back and the Old City laid out before you, you'll have
an amazing view from the Mount of Olives. The mountain is 872 meters (2,860 feet) high and
towers almost 60 meters (200 feet) above the Old City. This makes it one of the most beautiful
observation points in Jerusalem, in addition to being one of the city's most interesting sites.
Sometimes the place is filled with tour groups simply because this spot lends itself to discussions
about almost any historical subject, ranging from Abraham to Obama. You can even talk about
the future from this vantage point – the valley between the Mount of Olives and the Old City is
called the Valley of Josaphat, which means "God will judge." Adherents of the three Abrahamic
faiths believe that the mountain will be an important place in the Last Days. Observant Jews
believe that when the Messiah comes, all Jews will rise from the dead, but those who are buried
on the Mount of Olives will be the first to rise. Some Christians believe that Jesus will return to
Jerusalem at this very spot because this is where he ascended to heaven. The Muslims believe
that a slender bridge will connect the Temple Mount to the Mount of Olives, and that only the
righteous will be able to pass safely, while the wicked will fall off.

The view from the Mount of Olives.

3. Jewish cemetery

If you want to get away from the many groups who frequent the observation point, go down to the enormous cemetery that lies at the bottom of the observation area. Cemeteries hint at the importance of life more than anything else and provide insights into a society's attitude toward death, something that is especially true about this site, the world's oldest active Jewish cemetery. Jews have been buried here for many hundreds of years, with some of the graves dating back 2,500 years to the First Temple period.

Because death is considered impure in Judaism, Jews bury their dead as quickly as possible, and cemeteries are placed outside of the city. Death is considered so defiling that practicing Jews of the priestly caste (usually with last names like Cohen, Kahana, Katz, or Cahanovitc) won't enter a cemetery, even if it is a family member who is being buried. (According to the Bible, "Cohanim" are the descendants of Aaron, Moses' brother, who, along with his male descendants, was the priest of the Temple. Today, the last name Cohen is very common among Jews.) In the Bible, if a person was defiled by death (for example, by coming into direct contact with a corpse or staying in a house with one), the way to purify him was by burning a red heifer on the Mount of Olives, mixing the ashes with water, and dripping this mixture onto the defiled person.

Jews don't bury their dead in coffins, but wrap them in cloth before burying them underground. Thirty days after the burial, a gravestone is put up upon which the name, date of birth and death of the deceased is written. At many graves, you will see a place for a candle. It is customary to visit the grave every year on the anniversary of the death and light a candle for the departed soul. Notice that you will almost never see flowers on graves. Jews, especially

The Jewish cemetery.

Dominus Flevit Church.

The view from the window behind the altar.

observant ones, don't place flowers on graves but they do place small stones instead. This is not a religious commandment but a tradition - and that's why you'll hear a lot of different explanations for it. Some say that the stones are a way to mark the visit, which is why there are many stones on the graves of important people. Another explanation is that leaving a stone is a way to symbolically participate in the making of the headstone.

4. Dominus Flevit Church

Opening hours: 08:00-11:45, 14:30-17:00 (year around)
Entrance fee: Free

This little Franciscan church Dominus Flevit commemorates the place where Jesus wept, and hence its name, which translates from Latin as "the Lord wept." As he approached Jerusalem and saw the city, he wept over it and said, "If you, even you, had only known on this day what would bring you peace - but now it is hidden from your eyes. The days will come upon you when your enemies will build an embankment against you and encircle you and hem you in on every side. They will dash you to the ground, you and the children within your walls. They will not leave one stone on another, because you did not recognize the time of God's coming to you" (Luke 19:43-44).

On the right side of the path leading to the entrance of the church, there is a cave containing large stone chests. These are called "sarcophaguses," which literally means "flesh-eating stone" in Greek. That is because in ancient times, a corpse would be placed in a sarcophagus and, within a year, only the bones would remain. They would then be transferred to a smaller stone chest called an ossuary. At this site, there are Jewish names inscribed on the ossuaries, but on one of them is also an inscription of a Christian symbol. This is why the Franciscans believe that this burial place belonged to a Jewish–Christian community, the first believers in Jesus. It is important to stress the fact that Jesus was a Jew who preached to other Jews. Nowhere in the New Testament is it written that Jesus intended to formulate a new religion, and he never asked his followers to attend church every Sunday. Christianity, like Judaism and Islam, has adapted and changed over the years.

This small church was built in the year 1955 by Antonio Berluzzi, an Italian architect who designed many Franciscan churches in Israel. Berluzzi is known for his tendency to try and combine the biblical story connected to the site with the architectural design of the church and the landscape around it. The roof of the church was built in the shape of a teardrop and stone lachrymatories, or tear vials, were placed in the four corners. In the olden days, small bottles such as these were used to collect tears. Berluzzi managed to convey elements of Jesus' story within the church as well. In most churches, the altar points to the east – Jesus as a symbol of sunrise. In this church, the altar points to the west, the direction of the Old City. Behind the altar is a large window. If you stand in the center of the church, the metal cross points to the Dome of the Rock – the place where the Second Temple once stood, the temple whose destruction Jesus foretold. (It is important to note that the New Testament was written towards the end of the first century, after the destruction of the Second Temple.)

5. Church of Mary Magdalene
Opening hours: Tuesday and Thursday, 10:00–12:00
Entrance fee: Free

Since the church is open only two days a week for a couple of hours, it may be difficult to visit during this short window of time. But don't worry – the outside of the church is actually the most impressive thing to see. Its roof consists of golden onion-shaped domes, similar to the Kremlin domes in Moscow. That, along with the Orthodox crosses, reveals that this is a Russian church.

The church is named after Mary Magdalene, who was one of Jesus' disciples. She was present at his crucifixion and was also the first to discover his empty coffin and to meet Jesus after he came back to life. In Catholic Christianity, she has been understood to be a sinful woman who repented after meeting Jesus. Only in 1969 did the Church rescind the accusations they had charged her with. In the Eastern Orthodox Church she has always enjoyed a prominent role, and many churches are named after her.

As opposed to other churches on this tour that have a direct connection to events from the New Testament, this church has nothing to do with Mary Magdalene. It is actually connected to another woman – Elizabeth Feodorovna. Feodorovna was born in 1864, a princess from one of the oldest and most distinguished royal families of Germany. Her grandmother was Queen Victoria of England. Feodorovna was considered one of the most beautiful and kind-hearted women of her time. Many princes tried their luck but all were denied by her until she finally agreed to marry Grand Duke Sergei Alexandrovich, the brother of Czar Alexander III. In 1881, they visited Jerusalem and initiated and financed the building of the Church of Mary Magdalene.

Church of Mary Magdalene

The tomb of Elizabeth Feodorovna.

The princess fell in love with Jerusalem and wrote in her will that she wished to be buried at the church. In 1905, her husband, who was the governor of Moscow, was murdered by a Communist assassin. After his death, Feodorovna stopped eating meat, wore clothes of mourning, and became a nun. She visited her husband's assassin in prison and pleaded with him to show regret. She also pleaded with the Czar to pardon him, but her efforts did not bear fruit and the assassin was hanged. The princess sold her jewels and used the money to open a monastery in Moscow. Although she dedicated her life to helping the unfortunate, in 1918, after the Communist uprising, Lenin banished her from Moscow and had her executed. Feodorovna's body was smuggled to China, and in 1920, her bones were brought to their final resting place in Jerusalem. She is entombed in a glass coffin in the church, and her maid and one of her relatives are buried at her side.

The Differences Between Catholicism and Orthodoxy

The overwhelming majority of the churches in Jerusalem belong to either the Roman Catholic or the Eastern Orthodox Church. The rift between them began in the 11th century. In order to understand its source, we must return to the beginnings of Christianity. Jesus was crucified around the year 30 CE. For three hundred years, Christianity was a forbidden religion, until Constantine the Great legalized it in 324. But then the question was raised: What exactly is Christianity? Over time, different groups with different ideals had developed. After a series of seven councils (called the Ecumenical Councils, meaning the "inhabited world"), which were held between the years 325 and 787, the main articles of faith were decided upon, as well as prayers and Christian theology. In the first council in 325, it was ruled that Jesus and the Holy Father were equal in their essence and that they both have existed eternally. Those who believed that Jesus was born from God, his Father, were declared heretics. The decisions that were made in these seven councils are considered binding for both Catholics and Orthodox Christians. In 1054, the Catholics (then referred to as the Latin Church) demanded that the words "and (from) the Son" should be added to the phrase "the Holy Spirit proceeds from the Father" in the Nicene Creed. The Orthodox Christians refused. The division was caused not only by this theological disagreement but had many political reasons as well – power struggles between the Bishop of Rome (the Pope) and the emperor who sat in Constantinople (today's Istanbul). In addition, the Catholics claimed that the Pope in Rome was superior to the four patriarchs of Alexandria, Antioch, Jerusalem, and Constantinople. Another difference between them was language. On the eastern side of the Mediterranean Sea, the language of prayer was Greek, while on the western side, it was Latin. In recent years, there have been gestures of peace between the two branches and their relations have grown closer.

The Roman Catholic Church is more centralized, and all of its believers and organizations are subject to the Pope in Rome. The Eastern Orthodox Church is divided into 14 patriarchs, mainly according to countries. In Israel, most of the holdings of the Orthodox Church belong to the Greek Orthodox Church.

Christian Symbols in Jerusalem

In this booklet, I've only written about a small number of churches. While wandering through the city's streets, you will encounter many different Christian churches and institutions. These symbols will help you decipher whom they belong to (in addition to being an interesting bit of information in itself)

The Jerusalem Cross – This cross was used by the Crusaders and is also known as the Cross of Bethlehem. The four smaller crosses symbolize the nails that were driven into Christ's body and the four evangelists. This is a symbol you will see primarily on Catholic churches.

Taphos – The symbol of the Greek Orthodox Church is called "taphos" and is constructed from the Greek letters "tau" (T) and "phi" (□). These two letters spell out the word "tomb" or "sepulchre" in Greek, and they symbolize the sacred burial place of Jesus.

The Symbol of the Franciscans – The upper part features a crown symbolizing the Father and ruler of heaven, and underneath the crown a dove symbolizing the Holy Spirit. The bare arm belongs to Jesus and the sleeved one to St. Francis. On the palms of the hands you can see a small cut that symbolizes the nail in Christ's hand and the marks of the stigmata – the wounds where nails had pierced Christ's body (according to tradition, St. Francis was the first to have the stigmata wounds appear on his body). Below this is the Jerusalem cross. The inscription "S. Mons Sion in Jerusalem" refers to one of the main Franciscan sites in Jerusalem – Mount Zion.

The Papal Flag – Half of the flag is white, and the other half is yellow. Sometimes a pair of crossed keys are depicted on the white half. These are the keys to heaven, the symbol of the pope. This flag is flown above buildings belonging to Catholic countries and institutions.

The Greek Orthodox Flag – This flag features the taphos symbol in the middle of a red cross. A Greek flag is usually flying right next to it.

The Russian Orthodox Cross – This is the symbol of the Russian Church. The lower horizontal beam is at an angle, resulting in a left side that is higher up than the right. According to tradition, Jesus was crucified between two thieves. The one to Jesus' right, Dismas, was a penitent thief, while the other, Gestas, taunted him. Therefore, the beam points upwards on the side of the penitent thief and slopes downwards to symbolize the impenitent thief.

The Symbol of the Armenian Patriarch – It is constructed of the two first letters of the Armenian words for "holy" and "Jacob" (or "Santiago" in other languages): Ց (sourp) and ս (hagop). The Armenians wish to commemorate with this symbol both St. James, the disciple of Jesus, and James, the brother of Jesus who stood at the head of the Jewish community in Jerusalem.

The Coptic Cross – This is the symbol of the Copts, the Egyptian Christians.

Alpha-Omega – In the Greek alphabet, alpha is the first letter and omega the last. This symbolizes Jesus' saying, "I am the Alpha and the Omega, the beginning and the end" (Revelation 1:8). Even though this symbol contains Greek letters and is associated with the Eastern Orthodox Church, it's actually more common in the Roman Catholic Church.

Chi-Rho – These are two first letters of the word "Christos" (Messiah) in Greek. It is one of the oldest Christian symbols and is usually used by the Roman Catholic Church.

6. Gethsemane

Opening hours: April-September, 8:00-12:00, 14:00-18:00
October-March, 8:00-12:00, 14:00-17:00
Entrance fee: Free

The name Gethsemane comes from two Hebrew words - "gat" (press) and "shmanim" (oils). When the Bible was translated, the two words were accidentally written as one word. This is not the only mistake in the Bible's translation. The name Armageddon is actually two words in Hebrew - "Har Megiddo" (the mountain of Megiddo).

In the church's garden are some very old olive trees. It is difficult to estimate their exact age because the main trunks have died over time and new shoots have grown up around them. Researchers estimate that they are between seven hundred and one thousand years old. The Franciscans claim that one of the trees is two thousand years old - from the time of Jesus.

This church, like the other churches, is very new, having been built only ninety years ago. This gives rise to the question: Why is it that in Jerusalem, the cradle of Christianity, so many of the churches are new? Shouldn't most of the churches be at least two thousand years old?

Jesus was crucified in the year 30 CE, and the practice of Christianity was forbidden for three hundred years after that. During this time the building of churches was prohibited. Only after Constantine, the Roman emperor, converted to Christianity in 324 did his mother visit

Jerusalem and order the construction of the first churches. The invasion of the Holy Land by the Sasanian Empire in 614 and the Muslim conquest in 638 saw the destruction of many of these churches. Only when the Crusaders arrived in 1099 were the churches built anew. Two hundred years later, the Mamluks, an Islamic dynasty from Egypt, came and destroyed the churches once again. After the decline of the Ottoman Empire, during the British Mandate period, the churches were rebuilt for the third time – including the church before you.

This church honors one of the most difficult periods in Jesus' life. If the Mosque of the Ascension at the top of the Mount of Olives reminds us of Christ's divine aspect – his ascension to heaven – this place, at the lowest part of the Mount of Olives, reveals Christ's human side to

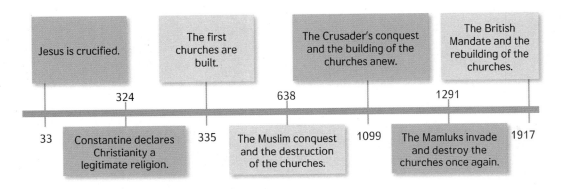

us. After Christ and his followers ate the Last Supper, they came to sleep in a cave in this area. Jesus could not sleep and asked three of his disciples to come and pray with him. Jesus prayed to the Father and asked, "Father, if you are willing, take this cup from me." Jesus knew that he would be crucified the next day and asked his Father for mercy. After the prayer, he saw that his disciples had not prayed with him like he asked but instead had fallen asleep (Luke 22: 39-46).

Antonio Berluzzi, who planned this church as well, designed the church to be gloomy in order to emphasize this dark event. When the base was rebuilt, remnants and part of the mosaic from the first church (built here in the 4th century) were uncovered. Berluzzi redesigned his plans of the church so that its contours would more closely resemble the ancient church that once stood here. Fragments from the 1,500-year-old mosaic were combined with the new mosaic on the floor of the church and protected by glass. The roof of the church has twelve domes, each one dedicated to a country that contributed money for the building of the church. The church was inaugurated in 1924, and its construction was made possible by the contributions of twelve nations that fought on both sides during World War I – thus earning the name "Church of All Nations." The most important place of the church is not the roof or the floor, but the stone that rests before the altar upon which Jesus prayed the night before his crucifixion.

The altar in the Gethsemane Church.

The twelve-domed roof.

The Tomb of the Virgin Mary.

7. The Tomb of the Virgin Mary

Opening hours: April–September, 5:00–12:00, 14:30–17:00
October–March, 6:00–12:00, 14:30–17:00
Entrance fee: Free

Many people pass by without noticing this church because it lies below street level. It's advisable to dedicate some of your time to visiting this church, which you can reach by taking the stairs leading down to it. The church commemorates the burial place of Mary, the mother of Jesus.

According to Christian theology, we die because we sin. Mary, mother of Jesus, did not sin, and therefore did not die. She fell asleep and her body was buried and she ascended – body and soul – to heaven. There are two different answers to the question, "Where was she buried?" According to the Catholics, she was buried in Ephesus in Turkey, and according to the Eastern Orthodox Church, she is buried in this church. Who is right? No one can say for sure. The New Testament does not state where Mary lived after Christ's crucifixion.

When you descend the dark staircase, you can tell it's an ancient church. As opposed to the newer churches on the Mount of Olives, this church dates back to the Crusader period, from the year 1130. On the way down to your right is a recess that contains two graves. According to tradition, these graves belong to Anna (Hannah) and Joachim, Mary's parents. Historians claim that this is actually the grave of Melisende, a Crusader queen. Melisende was the daughter of Baldwin II, King of Jerusalem during the Crusader period. He had no sons but he recognized his daughter's ability to rule and gave her his authority. After his death, Fulk V, Count of Anjou and Melisende's husband, tried to disinherit her from her title. However, she managed to overpower him with the help and support of the local church and the Crusaders who lived in the Kingdom of Jerusalem. Her son, Baldwin III, also conspired against her in an attempt to become the sole ruler. Despite the complex political situation with the Muslims who threatened the kingdom from without and the turbulent political currents from within, Melisende ruled for more than twenty years, between 1131 and 1153. William of Tyre, a historian who documented the Crusader period, wrote, "Melisende, the king's mother, was a woman of great wisdom who had much experience in all kinds of secular matters. She had risen so far above the normal status of women that she dared to undertake important measures." This was a great compliment at the time he was writing.

How is it possible that the grave of such an important woman became the graves of Anna and Joachim? The Eastern Orthodox Church did not approve of the Crusaders' conquest of their sites because they were Catholics and Western Europeans, and they felt that the Catholics viewed them as second-class Christians. In the Church of the Holy Sepulchre, which you will reach later on in the tour, there are benches on the Orthodox side on top of what were once graves of Crusader kings.

The visitors to the church usually come to visit the grave of Mary, which is in the central hall, and not because Melisende is buried here. In the past, this was a cave but its sides were dug out and a small chapel with a low roof was created. In the chapel there is an empty grave, since Mary's body and soul both ascended to heaven. The grave is protected by a glass wall because pilgrims used to break off pieces to take home as souvenirs. In the hall, there are a number of

The chapel where Melisende was buried.

altars that belong to various Christian groups – Greek Orthodox, Copts, Syriac Orthodox, Armenians, and even Catholics (although the Roman Catholic Church believes that Mary is buried in Turkey). The ownership of the church itself is exchanged daily between the Greek Orthodox and the Armenians.

8. The Lion's Gate – the Old City
The Lion's Gate is one of the seven gates of the Old City. There is another gate, the Gate of Mercy (the Golden Gate), but it is blocked. Jews and Christians believe that this gate will open on the day the Messiah arrives.

The Lion's Gate is named after the two lions (which were probably intended to be cheetahs) that are embossed on each side of the gate. This gate has been etched into the memories of Israelis and Jews, as it is the gate through which the paratroopers entered on June 7, 1967, the third day of the Six-Day War, on their way to the Wailing Wall and the Jewish Quarter after 19 years of Jordanian rule.

The Old City which you will now enter is very small - one kilometer in length and width. In this square kilometer, you will find the most sacred site to Jews around the world, one of the holiest sites in Christianity, and the third most important site in Islam. On top of that, there are at least fifty churches, chapels, and monasteries within these walls. There is no other place in the world that contains so many holy sites. Besides the sanctity of the city, there is also a lot of historical significance. Jerusalem has been conquered many times during the four thousand years of its existence. During the conquests and its rebuilding, the city has grown more than

OLD CITY OF JERUSALEM

The Lion's Gate.

twenty meters in height in some areas. Yehuda Amichai, one of Jerusalem's greatest poets, wrote in one of his poems that no one, not even the archaeologists, has ever seen Jerusalem naked. In the coming sites, you will discover a little of the Old City's never-ending richness.

The Old City is divided into four quarters – Jewish, Muslim, Christian, and Armenian. The Armenians received their own quarter because they were the first people to become Christian, back in 301 CE, and ever since then they have been coming to Jerusalem as pilgrims. Since the beginning of the 4th century, there has been a small Armenian community in Jerusalem. When the Crusaders came to Jerusalem, they defeated the Muslims and Jews who fought together on the same side and massacred them. The Crusaders did not harm the small Armenian community. Most of the Crusaders were men, and they married local women. The wife of Baldwin II (Queen Melisende's mother) was Armenian.

Most of the Armenians who live in Israel today are not the descendants of those pilgrims or of the Crusaders, but refugees from the Armenian genocide. During World War I, and especially during the year 1915, the Turkish murdered between a million to a million and a half Armenians. In the Armenian quarter, you will see posters calling for the recognition of the Armenian genocide.

The Lion's Gate leads to the Muslim quarter, which is the largest quarter. The total population of the Old City is about 36,000. Of these, 22,000 live in the Muslim quarter, 6,000 in the Jewish quarter, another 6,000 in the Christian quarter, and about 2,000 in the Armenian quarter. You might encounter other numbers, as each quarter strives to inflate its numbers. However, they all will agree that the Muslim quarter is the largest.

9. The Church of St. Anne

Opening hours: April–September, 8:00–12:00, 14:00–18:00
October–March, 8:00–12:00, 14:00–17:00
Entrance fee: NIS 7

Fifty meters from the Lion's Gate, on the right-hand side, is the Church of St. Anne. In the church's courtyard there is a little garden and an archeological site that is affiliated with the Pools of Bethesda. These pools were built 2,500–3,000 years ago and are the reservoirs for the waters of a small stream. Though there are no sources of water in Jerusalem other than the Gihon Spring, there are many reservoirs. These pools are important in Christianity because this is where Jesus healed a sick man (John 5:2-9). It is interesting that both of the miracles that Jesus performed in Jerusalem were connected to water. The other miracle was performed near the Pool of Siloam (John 9:1-7).

This church is one of the three Crusader churches that have been preserved in whole. It was built in the 12th century and, like other Crusader churches, is similar to a fortress. According to tradition, this is where Anna (Hannah) and Joachim lived and also where their daughter, Mary, mother of Jesus, was born.

This church has excellent acoustics and if you have some time, it is recommended to wait for a group of pilgrims (or some other group) to raise their voices in song.

This church belongs to an order of French Catholics called the White Fathers (after the color of its followers' robes).

The Pools of Bethseda.

The inside of this Crusader church.

Via Dolorosa

The phrase "Via Dolorosa" means "the path of suffering" in Latin. The fourteen stations begin with the place where Pontius Pilate, the Roman prefect of Judea, condemned Jesus Christ to death. The path ends in the place where Jesus was crucified and buried – today the inside of the Church of the Holy Sepulchre. In the past the Via Dolorosa followed other routes; for example, it used to begin at Mount Zion or at the Jaffa Gate. The path as we know it today was created by the Franciscans in 1342, but pilgrims in the 14th to the 17th centuries described different stations along the same path. Only during the 19th century were the path and its stations consolidated as they are today.

Groups of pilgrims, especially Roman Catholic and Eastern Orthodox ones, often rent a large wooden cross and bear it while praying and singing hymns on their way along the path. On Friday afternoons you can join the Franciscans while they make their way through the Via Dolorosa (April-September at 16:00, October-March at 15:00).

The stations are marked on a large metal board with Roman numerals. The opening hours are not very consistent; many stations are closed most of the time.

The Stations of the Cross

The First Station – The place of Jesus' trial. In the past, the Antonia fortress stood in the place where, according to tradition, Jesus was sentenced by Pontius Pilate (Matthew 17:11-14). Today, this is a Muslim school for boys that usually does not allow visitors on the premises.

The Second Station – Two churches (right across the first station) commemorate the place where Jesus was whipped and given the cross to bear in the area that belongs to the Franciscans (John 19:1-2).

10. The Convent of the Sisters of Zion
Opening hours: 8:00-17:00
Entrance fee: NIS 8

In the past, it was thought that the circular area outside of the convent was the place where Pontius Pilate said, "Behold the man." This statement referred to the idea that Jesus was the man the Jews wished to have crucified, and that is why the arch is named Ecce Homo ("Behold the man" in Latin). Today it is known that the gate was built a hundred years after the crucifixion of Jesus. The plan for building the convent was set in motion by Marie-Alphonse Ratisbonne, a French Jew who converted to Christianity and consecrated the convent in 1868. Despite the fact that it is a modern building and not part of the Via Dolorosa, it is still worth visiting because you can descend to an underground reservoir that was built around Herod's time (two thousand years ago). The phrase "historical depth" has real physical meaning here.

The Third Station - This station is at the intersection of the streets Via Dolorosa and the Guy (Wadi), and it serves to commemorate the place where Jesus fell the first time under the weight of the cross. There are three stations along the Via Dolorosa that mark the places where Jesus fell, but none of them are mentioned in the Scriptures.

On the other side of the street you can find the Austrian Hospice. Contrary to what many believe, this is not a hospital, but a hostel. You can ring the bell to be let in. The hospice is an Austrian island of quiet in the heart of the bustling Muslim quarter. If you climb up to the roof, you will be rewarded with a great view of the Old City. In the cafeteria you can enjoy a sip of Viennese coffee and eat apple strudel while the emperor Franz Joseph stares at you from his portrait on the wall.

The Fourth Station - This is where Jesus met his mother. This station is also not mentioned in the Scriptures.

The Fifth Station - This is where Simon of Cyrene helped Jesus bear the cross (Luke 23:26). On the wall is a stone where, according to tradition, you can see the handprint of Jesus from when he leaned on the wall on his way to the crucifixion.

Across from the fifth station is a restaurant called Abu Shukri. This is one of the best places to eat hummus in Jerusalem.

The Ecce Homo Arch.

Up to this point, we have mostly toured Christian sites. You can now choose to continue along the Via Dolorosa or to visit the Wailing Wall and the Dome of the Rock instead, completing the Via Dolorosa part of the tour later.

(To continue along the Via Dolorosa, go to page 38.)

11. The Kotel (the Wailing Wall or the Western Wall)

If you ask Israelis what the Wailing Wall is, many of them will tell you that it is the most sacred place to Jews in the world and that it was part of the Second Temple. Both of these beliefs are incorrect. Two thousand years ago when the Temple was still standing, the Western Wall had no meaning whatsoever. In order to understand what the Western Wall is, you must go back three thousand years. King Solomon built the First Temple. The Temple stood on the top of Mount Moriah, on the stone from which Jews believed the world was created, known as the Foundation Stone. This is also the place where Abraham almost sacrificed his son Isaac. The Temple stood for five hundred years until the Babylonians conquered Jerusalem and destroyed the Temple in 586 BCE. The Holy Ark and the Ten Commandments, which were in the Temple, vanished with its destruction, and the Jews were expelled from the Land of Israel. Seventy years later, the Jews were permitted to return and they built the Second Temple. The Temple was renovated a number of times until King Herod (who ruled between the years 37 BCE and 4 BCE) decided to rebuild the Temple. He had a problem though - the Temple stood on the peak of a mountain where there was only limited space. King Herod, who was known for his massive building projects, decided that he would build four huge supporting walls around the mountain peak and thus transform it into a great level platform. On this man-made platform he rebuilt the Temple. The Western Wall is actually a small part (about one-seventh) of one of the large supporting walls. In the year 70 CE, during the Jewish rebellion against the Romans, Jerusalem was conquered and the Temple was destroyed. After the rebellion Jews were not permitted to return to the area of the Temple, and the Kotel was the closest that Jews could come to that area. The Western Wall, and not the Southern or Eastern Walls, is the most sacred because the Temple – and within it the Holy of Holies – was not in the center of the platform, but was built closer to the western side. Up until today, the most sacred place to Jews is the Temple Mount itself.

The Temple that Herod built was the holiest place in the Roman Empire. Non–Jews were also permitted to ascend to the platform, but just to the farthest part of the Temple. Only Jews were allowed to come closer to the Temple; and closer than that, only men; and even closer than that, only the "Cohanim" (priests); and the Holy of Holies – the holiest of rooms within the Temple – could only be entered by the High Priest himself, and that only once a year on the Day of Atonement (Yom Kippur), the most important day in the Jewish calendar. And what was in the Holy of Holies? In the First Temple it contained the Ark and the Ten Commandments, but in the Second Temple the room was empty – or more precisely, it was full of the Shekhinah, the Divine Presence of God. Believers – Jewish, Christian, and Muslim alike – all need holy places (such as mosques, churches, synagogues, graves, and holy stones), but in the end they all believe in one God who cannot be seen and whose image cannot be depicted. So it actually makes sense that the Holy of Holies was an empty room.

The Western Wall today is actually a part of an open synagogue, which is why men and

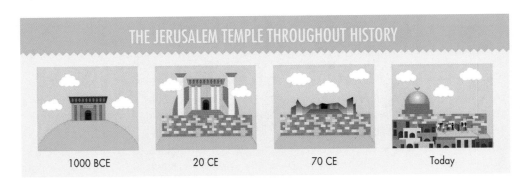

THE JERUSALEM TEMPLE THROUGHOUT HISTORY

| 1000 BCE | 20 CE | 70 CE | Today |

women are separated like in many synagogues. There is a tradition, probably only a few hundred years old, where you're supposed to write a prayer upon a piece of paper and place it between the rocks of the Kotel. In fact, you can also write an email, a text message, or a letter to the Kotel, and the office of the Kotel Rabbinate will place the prayer in the Kotel for you. But if you're already here, bring a pencil and a piece of paper with you and just do it yourself. Even non–Jews leave prayers. In 2008, there was a small scandal when the prayer left by the then US presidential candidate, Barack Obama, was taken out by a young Israeli. Its contents were published in an Israeli newspaper, a prime example of Israeli chutzpah that went too far.

Every few months, the Rabbi of the Kotel removes all of the prayers to make space for new ones. But because the name of God appears in many of the prayers, they can't be thrown away and are instead buried on the Mount of Olives.

A Little Bit About the Haredi Jews' Garb and Customs

The Haredi Jews are Orthodox Jews who follow all of the commandments of the halacha - the laws and customs of Judaism that have evolved over thousands of years. Haredi Jews make up about ten percent of the Jewish population in Israel - some 700,000 people in all. The first thing that you notice about them, of course, is their garb. The long black clothing stands out. That is also one of its purposes, to differentiate them from their surroundings. Another reason is modesty. Like many other religious groups, they also make sure to cover up.

Jews didn't always dress this way. King Solomon didn't wear black clothing and a fur hat in the middle of summer. This way of dressing began around two hundred years ago in Eastern Europe. These clothes serve as a kind of uniform. In the same way that army uniforms immediately single out a soldier and show his rank and position, Haredi clothing singles out the Haredi Jew. There are special outfits for the Sabbath and for regular weekdays, for married and for single people, and for different geographical origins. You might first think that they are wearing uniform black attire, but a closer look will reveal the differences between the outfits. Some wear long black jackets, others dark blue; some wear tall hats and others shorter ones; some wear black socks, while others wear white ones; and some married women cover their hair, while others wear wigs.

Sidelocks

One of the main differences between Judaism and Christianity is that Christians believe Jesus is the Messiah and follow his teachings. Judaism, on the other hand, centers around the halacha, an elaborate system of rules that Jews are supposed to adhere to. The Ten

Commandments are the most well-known laws, but there are actually 613 commandments laid out in the Jewish Bible.

Judaism is a religion of rules and decrees. There are thousands of rules that cover nearly every single aspect of life. Many passages in the Bible are considered binding rules. In the book of Leviticus, Chapter 19, Verse 27, it is written "You shall not round (shave) the corners of your heads." The origin of this prohibition is probably lies in the fact that other "pagan" peoples were in the practice of shaving around their heads. It is not written that you must grow out your hair, only that you should not shave it, but religious Jews customarily grow out their sidelocks as a sign of piety. The sidelocks, like the clothing, indicate which religious group the person belongs to. Some place their sidelocks inside their hats, some tuck them behind the ears, some have short sidelocks, and others let their long curled sidelocks blow with the wind.

Tefillin (Phylacteries) – Religious Jewish men pray three times a day. The Shacharit, or morning prayer, is when they put on the tefillin, which are two small boxes attached to leather straps – one bound to the forehead and the other wound around the arm. There is a small parchment rolled up inside the boxes that has a number of passages from the Bible written on it, including the passage that explains the reason for the tefillin: "And you shall bind them for a sign upon your hand, and they shall be as frontlets between your eyes" (Deuteronomy 6:8).

What exactly are frontlets? No one really knows the meaning of the word, but 2,000 year old tefillin were found in the Judean Desert, proving that the tefillin used back then were similar to the tefillin used today.

Tallit – When Jews pray you will notice that they cover themselves with a shawl. A tallit is the Jewish prayer shawl. It is made usually of wool. There are two kinds of tallitot (the plural of tallit) – one that observant Jews will cover themselves with when they pray, and another one which they wear under their shirt. You will see the four tassels hanging outside the shirt. Wearing a tallit is one of the biblical commandments: "Speak to the Israelites and say to them: 'Throughout the generations to come you are to make tassels on the corners of your garments⬜ You will have these tassels to look at and so you will remember all the commands of the Lord'" (Numbers 15:38-9).

12. Visiting the Temple Mount

Opening hours: Summer: Sunday-Thursday, 8:00-11:30, 13:30-14:30
Winter: Sunday-Thursday, 7:30-10:00, 12:30-13:30

The Temple Mount is closed during Muslim holidays. It's recommended to check with the Kotel police station prior to visiting (02 622 6250).

Entrance fee: Free

Important: Wear modest attire; bringing prayer books, alcohol, or weapons is prohibited. You cannot exit from the same gate that you entered.

While waiting in line to enter the Temple Mount, you will see a sign in Hebrew and English asking Jews not to ascend to the Temple Mount. There are some Jews (including the Rabbi of the Kotel) who claim that the exact location of the Temple, including the Holy of Holies, isn't known. Only the High Priest was allowed to enter the Holy of Holies on the Day of Atonement, and if other Jews accidentally trespass on the Holy of Holies, it would be a sin. This is why some believe that it is better to simply avoid visiting the place and not run the risk of committing that sin. On the other hand, there are Jews who wish to pray in the holiest place in the world for Jews, who say that the location of the Temple can be inferred. Today, Jews and Christians are not allowed to pray on the Temple Mount because the area is under the control of the Waqf, the organization in charge of Islamic holy sites.

After a routine security check, you will walk over a wooden bridge. Before you reach the end of the bridge and enter the Temple Mount, have a look at the Kotel on your left. This is an excellent vantage point for taking pictures and allows you to understand the crux of the Israeli-Arab conflict. The Western Wall is a supporting wall on the platform upon which the Dome of the Rock and the Al-Aqsa Mosque stand. You cannot separate these holy places.

Al-Aqsa Mosque
Today, non-Muslims are not permitted to enter the Al-Aqsa Mosque.

Jerusalem is mentioned in the Bible more than 600 times and about 150 times in the New Testament. Jerusalem isn't mentioned in the Quran at all. Not even once. Jerusalem has served as the capital of the Jewish people for hundreds of years and as the Crusader's capital for a hundred years. The Muslim empires chose to have Cairo, Damascus and Baghdad as their capitals, but never Jerusalem. So how did Jerusalem become the third most important city to Islam, after Mecca and Medina?

The 17th sura (chapter) of the Quran tells the story of Mohammed's night journey. Mohammed rides Al-Buraq, a fabled animal with the body of a horse, the wings of a bird, and a woman's head, to the farthest mosque and from there he ascends to heaven and receives the

Al-Aqsa Mosque.

The Dome of the Rock.

commandment of prayer. The meaning of "farthest" in Arabic is "Al-Aqsa" – and that is the name of the mosque with the gray dome. The mosque was built in the year 705 CE, but only fragments remain of the original building. Most of the building you see today was built in the 11th century.

The Dome of the Rock
Entrance to non-Muslims is forbidden.

The Dome of the Rock is the most impressive building in the Old City. Unlike other important buildings that were destroyed and rebuilt or remodeled and changed, most of this building is original. The Dome of the Rock was built in 692 CE and is the oldest Islamic building still standing today. It is named after the natural rock in its center, which is considered very important in Judaism as well. The Jews believe that this the Foundation Stone, the stone from which the world was made and upon which Abraham almost sacrificed his son Isaac. The First and Second Temple were built exactly upon this stone. The Muslims believe that Mohammed ascended to heaven after standing upon this stone. The stone wanted to fly with Mohammed to heaven, but the angel Gabriel threw a rock at the stone, causing a cave to open up under it.

Exit through the Juneima Gate and
return to the fifth station on the Via Dolorosa.

The Sixth Station - Jesus meets Veronica, who wipes his face clean of blood and sweat. To her surprise, a likeness of Jesus' face appears on the veil she used. Legends say that people who have touched the cloth were healed. This story does not appear in the New Testament.

The Seventh Station - Jesus falls for the second time, stumbling when he leaves through the "Gate of Judgment," the gate through which those who were sentenced to death left the city. There is also no reference to this story in the New Testament.

The Eighth Station - Jesus speaks to the women of Jerusalem. The location of this station was only decided upon in the 19th century, but this event does in fact appear in the New Testament. Jesus turns to the women of Jerusalem and asks that they weep not for him, but for themselves (Luke 23:27-31). The letters "IC" and "XC" are inscribed on the stone set in the wall of a Greek Orthodox convent. These are the first and last letters of the Greek words "IHCOYC" (Jesus) and "XPICTOC" (Christ). Underneath them is the Greek word "NIKA" (victory).

 Please note: It's easy to miss the right-hand turn to the stairs that lead up to the ninth station.

The Ninth Station – Jesus falls for the third time. This is the last station outside of the Church of the Holy Sepulchre. I highly recommend visiting this station because it contains one of the most magical places in the Old City. Leave a dollar or two at the entrance, turn on the light and descend the steps to a two-thousand-year-old underground pool. The water that fills the pool today is rain water.

13. The Roof of the Church of the Holy Sepulchre

The church's roof acts a sort of introduction to the church itself. It looks as though the Church of the Holy Sepulchre didn't have enough room inside for all its wealth of history, stories, and traditions. History worked its way up to the areas in front of the church and to its roof.

There is a small Ethiopian village on the roof of the church. The Ethiopians used to own a small area inside of the church, but a few hundred years ago they were forced to give it up and moved into small cottages on the roof of the church. The name of the place is Dir Al-Sultan, which means "the sultan's monastery." But rather than referring to an Ottoman sultan, it's in

CHURCH OF THE HOLY SEPULCHRE

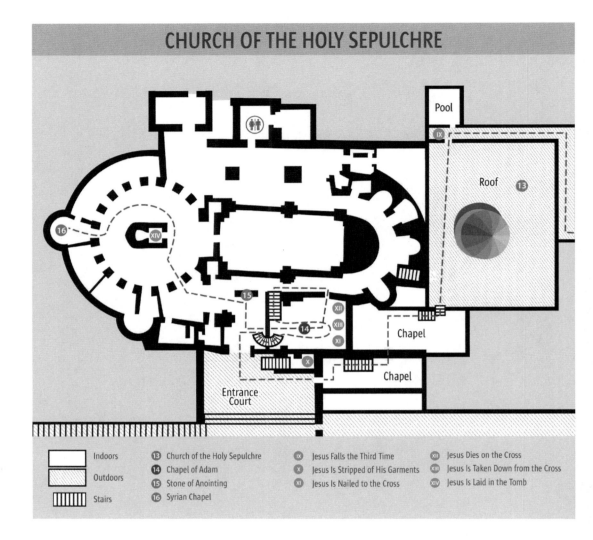

| | Indoors |
| | Outdoors |
| Stairs |

13 Church of the Holy Sepulchre
14 Chapel of Adam
15 Stone of Anointing
16 Syrian Chapel

IX Jesus Falls the Third Time
X Jesus Is Stripped of His Garments
XI Jesus Is Nailed to the Cross

XII Jesus Dies on the Cross
XIII Jesus Is Taken Down from the Cross
XIV Jesus Is Laid in the Tomb

homage to King Solomon. The Ethiopians believe that when the Queen of Sheba returned from her visit to King Solomon, she carried the future king of Ethiopia in her womb. The Ethiopians were one of the first people to convert to Christianity and have had a presence in Jerusalem since the 4th century.

A thousand years ago, during the Crusader period, there was a large room here, and you can still see the pillars that supported the roof of the edifice. From the roof, you can descend to the faade of the church by passing through the Ethiopian chapels. Note that it is quite dark in the chapels.

The roof of the Church of the Holy Sepulchre.

The Façade of the Church of the Holy Sepulchre

Opening hours: April-September, 5:30-21:00

October-March, 4:30-19:30

Entrance fee: Free

The Church of the Holy Sepulchre is the holiest place for most Christians around the world. Wars, earthquakes, and the many additions and changes made to this house of worship in the last 1,700 years have lessened its impressiveness. The real beauty lies in its story.

The church was built in the year 335 CE by Helena, the mother of Constantine, who according to tradition was the one to locate the site of the crucifixion. Very little remains of the original structure of the church. The external façade of the church that you see today is mostly from the Crusader period (the 12th century).

The church contains two very important sites - Golgotha (or Calvary), the place where Jesus Christ was crucified, and his grave. Many imagine Golgotha as a mountain outside of the Old City, but that's not the case; it lies within the church.

This church is also special because it doesn't belong to any one of the specific Christian denominations. Instead, it is divided between six different denominations. Most of the church is in the hands of the Roman Catholics (Franciscans), the Eastern Orthodox, and the Armenians.

The small remainder is split between the Syriac Orthodox, the Copts, and the Ethiopians.

The different denominations never got along with each other. In 1852, after hundreds of years of quarrels, clashes, and wars, the Ottomans forced them to sign a status quo agreement in which they swore to accept the current arrangement. The agreement was very detailed and not only included the division of the territory, but also who is allowed to pray where and when, and even who has the right to turn on the lights. The best-known symbol of the status quo is the Immovable Ladder, a wooden ladder leaning against the faᵡade of the church underneath the upper right window. The Armenians set the ladder there because there were periods in which the Muslims closed the church with the monks still inside. In order to get food, the Armenian monks would climb out the window and down the ladder to a small porch where there was a rope. The Armenians in the city would place food and drink in a pail on the ground, which the monks would haul up using the rope. Today the church is open every day, and there is no use for the ladder. So why is it still there? Because that is what is written in the status quo agreement: the Armenians have the right to place a ladder there. So even if it were to rot or break, the Armenians would replace it with a new one.

To the many visitors, the conflicts and squabbles between the different denominations seem petty and unworthy of the place. Even if there is truth in this, it's important to remember that for these denominations this is the holiest place in the world. They have inhabited this building for hundreds of years, and no one wants to give in on anything or have anyone impinge on their rights.

The faade of the Church of the Holy Sepulchre.

The Immovable Ladder.

And what about the Protestants? The Protestants came to Jerusalem 130 years ago and claimed that the Church of the Holy Sepulchre was built in the wrong place – because Jesus was a Jew and Jews do not bury their dead within the city, and since the church lies within the Old City, the grave cannot be there. The Protestants are right. Jews, as we have said, bury their dead outside of the city's borders. The Protestants simply pulled the rug out from beneath millions of believers who have come to the church for hundreds of years. The Protestants may have been right about the burial, but they were wrong about the city. The church has been within the city's borders for the last five hundred years, but two thousand years ago, in Jesus' time, that territory was outside of the city. Thus it's quite possible that Jesus was crucified and buried there. Despite that, the Protestants, who have no claim on the church, have found themselves an alternative place. Groups of Protestant believers come to a beautiful garden that lies outside of the Damascus Gate. To the Protestants, the exact location where Jesus was buried, fell, or prayed on a rock is not as important as the atmosphere – and in the Garden Tomb there is indeed a quiet and peaceful atmosphere.

The Church of the Holy Sepulchre is locked every night and opened early in the morning. Like everything about the church, even something as simple and supposedly routine as this has a surprising story behind it.

Saladin conquered Jerusalem in 1187. He took the keys from the Christians and gave them to two Muslim families - the Joudehs and the Nusseibehs - and for the last eight hundred years, they have been responsible for opening the church. Every morning (5:30 in the summer, 4:30 in the winter), representatives from the Eastern Orthodox, the Roman Catholics, and the Armenians who sleep inside the church meet in front of a door inside the building. Only the

Orthodox representative can open the small window in the door. Every morning, a different denomination is allowed to pass a small ladder through the window. A member of the Joudeh family that has the keys hands them to a member of the Nusseibeh family, who then climbs up the ladder to open the lock. After that, the Nusseibeh family member climbs down the ladder to open the doors of the church and returns the keys to the Joudeh family member. At night, there is a locking ceremony in which these same steps are repeated, simply in the reverse order.

What You Should Know Before Visiting the Church

All the noise and commotion caused by the numerous tour groups are a source of great disappointment for many visitors. "The place feels more like a market than a holy site" is something I've heard many times. So to avoid the crowds, try to come in the afternoon, at night, or before breakfast. If you do come during the busy hours, summon up all your patience and try to see through the commotion to the wonders of the place. Two billion people from all around the world believe that in this place, Jesus, the son of God, a Jew who lived two thousand years ago, sacrificed himself for all of humanity.

Sites Within the Church

The first thing that you'll notice within the church is the stone that many visitors kneel before and that many kiss. We will return to this stone later, but in order to keep to the chronological order, turn right and climb up the steep stairs. The stairs go up to Golgotha or Calvary (which means "skull" in Aramaic and Latin, respectively).

In the area of Golgotha, there are four more stations of the Via Dolorosa. The stations that are within the church aren't marked like the ones that are located outside.

The Tenth Station – You can only view this station through the window immediately on the right. This is the place where Roman soldiers stripped Jesus of his clothes.

The Eleventh Station – Jesus was nailed to the cross by the soldiers near where the Latin altar now stands. The mosaic on the wall depicts the scene of the crucifixion.

The Twelfth Station – The most important station in Golgotha is the place where, according to Christian belief Jesus died for the sins of humanity. There is usually a line of people kneeling beneath the altar and kissing the stone upon which Jesus was crucified.

The Thirteenth Station – This station is located between the eleventh and twelfth stations. It marks the place where Jesus's body was taken down from the cross. The station is commemorated by a statue of Mary, her heart pierced with a silver dagger representing grief. The statue is protected by glass because someone once stole the crown that was on her head.

> ❗ *Go down the straight staircase and turn right, and then right again into the chapel located beneath Golgotha.*

14. The Chapel of Adam

In the window behind the altar there is glass through which you can see a crack in the stone. A relatively new belief, dating from the Crusader period, says that when Jesus died on the cross – which was right above this spot – there was an earthquake and Jesus' blood dripped through the crack. The blood touched the bones of Adam, the first man, who was buried here (there are no bones here today). Was Adam really buried here? Probably not, but there is still an interesting theological connection between Jesus and Adam. Adam was born pure but when he ate the fruit from the tree of knowledge, he was burdened by original sin. Jesus, through his death upon the cross, atoned for original sin and made salvation possible for humanity.

Two benches inside the chapel (that you are welcome to sit on) have actually been placed on top of the tombs of Crusader kings. Two hundred years ago, there was a fire in the church that probably began because of a drunken monk. During the fire, a great part of the church was destroyed and the Eastern Orthodox monks took the opportunity to destroy the tombstones of the Crusaders (who were Roman Catholic) and place benches over them.

 Exit through the opening between the two benches, heading towards the stone at the entrance that you saw many pilgrims kiss.

15. The Stone of Anointing

The stone you see here is called the Stone of Anointing. Beneath it is believed to be the rock upon which Jesus' body was anointed with oil after it was removed from the cross and before the burial.

This stone is not a station on the Via Dolorosa, but it is still of great importance. The meaning of the word Christ is actually "anointed with oil" in ancient Greek. The word "Messiah" in Hebrew (Mashiach) also means "anointed in oil." Because Jews do not believe in Jesus, the name for Christians in Hebrew is Nazarenes (Notzrim), which means "those from the city of Nazareth." (In the same way, Jews are called so because of their origin from the kingdom of Judea, the mountains around Jerusalem.)

Many pilgrims kiss this stone and sometimes pass candles, souvenirs, and cloths over it. In the Eastern Orthodox Church, there is a belief that sacredness can pass from one object to another.

Jesus' Grave – The Fourteenth Station

Jesus was buried in a cave, but when the church was built, the cave was destroyed. A rotunda, a circular building, was built instead with the grave in its center. A long line winds around the grave, but the grave is empty. Jesus was crucified on a Friday, and the grave was found empty on Sunday. Jesus came back to life and walked on Earth for forty days until he ascended to heaven from the Mount of Olives. So why do people stand in line to see an empty grave? The significance of this station, the fourteenth station on the Via Dolorosa, is that this is where Jesus conquered death.

> ❗ *On the other side of the entrance to the grave is a small chapel that belongs to the Copts and, across from it, a Syriac Orthodox chapel.*

16. The Syrian Chapel

This place looks a bit neglected: its walls are darkened with charcoal, the altar is partially ruined, and the floor isn't paved. Many visitors skip this chapel. The Syriac Orthodox Church believes that this is where Joseph of Arimathea, the man who donated his grave plot to Jesus, is buried. Actually, the cave to the right of the altar is the historical site. This simple cave is in fact a burial site from the period of the Second Temple, Jesus' period. It proves that the Protestants' claim is wrong since this site was a Jewish cemetery two thousand years ago. And it is important because it shows what a Jewish grave looked like back then. Two thousand years ago there was no church here, there were no monks or Russian tourist groups, but only a handful of Jews who believed that the person buried here was the Messiah. Who knows, maybe Jesus really was buried in this cave.

Inside Jesus' grave.

17. Lutheran Church of the Redeemer

Opening hours: Monday-Saturday, 9:00-15:00; closed on Sundays
Entrance fee: Free
Observation tower and Excavation: NIS 15

The churches in Jerusalem, as you might have already noticed, are not only full of history but also visitors, candles, incense, statues, and icons. The Lutheran Church of the Redeemer is Protestant, as its name indicates, and relatively new, so it doesn't have many decorations. Protestant churches – and there are only two such churches in the Old City – often have a simpler and cleaner aesthetic. The church also offers the most beautiful view in the Old City. A hundred and seventy-eight steps lead to the top of the bell tower, the highest in the city.

The height of the bell tower is an indication of the "competition" that existed in the city between the European powers in the last half of the 19th century. As the Ottoman Empire slowly crumbled, the European powers consented to help it in exchange for more tolerance and special rights to build churches in the Old City. The Germans were granted the right to build three churches in Jerusalem as a result of the good relations they enjoyed with the Ottoman Empire in the years that preceded the First World War.

18. Jaffa Gate

Jerusalem has much to offer, but there is one important thing that it lacks – a port. For thousands of years, Jaffa, which is located 80 kilometers away, was the naval gateway to Jerusalem. From the Jaffa Gate begins the Jaffa Road, which leads all the way west to the coast.

Within the city walls of Jaffa there was once a Jerusalem Gate that faced the east. The road between Jaffa and Jerusalem was the first to be paved in the Land of Israel and today it's called Highway 1 (the road between Jerusalem and Tel Aviv).

Jerusalem has passed hands dozens of times throughout history – King David conquered the city by entering via a mysterious waterway; when the Crusaders came, inspired by Joshua's conquest of Jericho, they circled the walls hoping that they might fall. But it is especially the British entry into the city through the Jaffa Gate, at the end of World War I in 1917, that seems to be the most fitting story to end our tour with.

The Ottomans knew that the British strength was greater than theirs, so they decided to abandon the city in order to avoid battles that could destroy the sacred sites. On the night of December 8, the Ottoman forces withdrew from Jerusalem and retreated to Jericho. On the morning of December 9, Hussein Effendi, the mayor of Jerusalem, together with a delegation of the city's nobles and a white flag, traveled westward until they encountered two British soldiers and surrendered. They didn't know that they had surrendered to two cooks who had gotten lost on their way to buy eggs. When they continued, they met two sergeants who refused to accept their surrender, while, in the meantime, the two cooks found their way back to camp and reported the Ottoman delegation to their officers. One of these, Brigadier General Watson, agreed to accept the delegation and their surrender but his officer, Major General John Shea, canceled the surrender and demanded that they surrender once more, this time to him. General Allenby, commander of the Allied forces, canceled that surrender yet again and demanded that he be the one to accept the surrender. On December 11, there was a fifth and last surrender ceremony. General Allenby arrived on horseback at the Jaffa Gate, but when he reached the gate, he dismounted his horse as a gesture to the holy city and entered on foot, not as a general and a conqueror, but as a simple pilgrim.

Jaffa Gate